BARRIER REEF REFLECTIONS

BARRIER REEF REFLECTIONS

AUB PODLICH

with photographs by
RON and NGAIRE GALE
DON and JENNIFER COWIE

LEFT: Whitehaven Beach and Hill Inlet, Whitsunday Island

To our dear friend Fergus

from

Tom & Muriel

1995

His promises give life.

Lutheran Publishing House

Graphic Design by Graeme Cogdell

First printing August 1990

National Library of Australia Cataloguing-in-Publication data

Podlich, Aubrey, 1946-
  Barrier Reef reflections.

  ISBN 0 85910 551 2.

  1. Christian poetry, Australian. 2. Great Barrier Reef Region (Qld.) — Poetry.
  I. Gale, Ron. II. Title.

A821.3

Printed by Griffin Press, Adelaide.

Published by Lutheran Publishing House,
205 Halifax Street, Adelaide, South Australia. LPH 90-487

INTRODUCTION

In Queensland's north, two distinct and unique natural areas run roughly parallel to one another for many hundreds of kilometres, attracting thousands of admiring visitors each year. The one, a glorious remnant of a once-expansive green wilderness, today clothes mainly the jagged spine and sweeping ribs of the Great Dividing Range. The other, a vast jewel largely intact, sprawls along the Queensland coast for more than 2,000 kilometres, mostly submerged under the aqua waters of the Pacific Ocean. Together, they feature more living creatures in fragile, complex relationships than do any of the other habitats on the living planet earth. These two magnificent jewels are the World Heritage areas of our tropical rainforests, and the Great Barrier Reef.

Neither rainforest nor reef is one uniform and unbroken wall of green trees or coloured coral; there are many forests, many reefs — pockets, chains, and islands of trees or coral in broken, irregular groupings, some small, others extensive. They stretch, the one on land, the other at sea, all the way from the tip of Cape York to near Gladstone in central Queensland. No books, words, or photographs adequately capture the wonder of these magnificent expanses.

The Barrier Reef itself is not one, but many. More than 2,900 separate reefs are scattered in the incredibly clear, relatively shallow, blue and green tropical ocean from the Gulf of Papua in the north to Lady Elliot Island, below the Tropic of Capricorn. Thrusting up among the reefs are the heads of more than 540

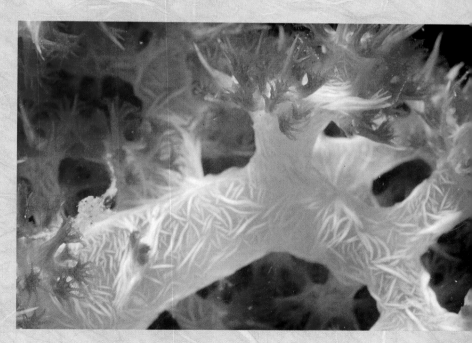

LEFT: *Hardy Reef, Great Barrier Reef*
UPPER RIGHT: *Panorama from The Fort, Horseshoe Bay, Magnetic Island*
LOWER RIGHT: *Intricate patterns of the teddy bear coral (dendronephthya)*

high continental islands, some heavily vegetated, and most with their own garland of fringing reefs. Because many of the resorts are situated on these islands, the tourists' usual experience of the Reef is of the fringing reefs around such continental islands.

Fringing reefs themselves are magnificent, complex, and varied. Yet they form only part of an intricate chain of reefs and islands so vast that it covers more than 230,000 square kilometres and is one of the few living complexes visible from the moon. Individual reefs range in size from 100 square kilometres to tiny coral outcrops, each one living, growing, changing as a dynamic community in this maze of channels, sandbars, lagoons,

and coral-fragment islands called cays, and all ministered to by the interactions of sunshine, currents, tides, and winds.

Tourists are sometimes surprised and disappointed that the Great Barrier Reef is not visible from the mainland. For the most part, the reefs begin more than 32 kilometres from the shore, and extend right to the lip of the continental shelf, in places 260 kilometres offshore. However, in the Daintree area, visitors may observe the rarest of natural wonders, known only at two other locations in the world. There, extensive coral reefs meet tropical rainforest, separated only by the magnificent sweep of curving beach. At Daintree, the mountains rising sharply from the beach provide only a small watershed for the fierce summer rains, and shed directly into the ocean less of the fresh water that is toxic to coral. Conditions are thus suitable for coral reefs close inshore.

Even the tiny glimpses we get of individual reefs through snorkelling, diving, or viewing from the

UPPER LEFT: *Fern leaves, Mulgrave Shire*
LOWER LEFT: *Purtaboi Island off Mission Beach*

traditional 'glass-bottomed' boat, reveal a bewildering and unbelievable kaleidoscope of living creatures, colours, and patterns. In such a truly alien world we struggle, humbled, for adequate words. Such an incredible number and variety of the most vividly coloured fish! So many shapes, forms, textures, and hues of coral! In fact, there are more than 2,000 species of fish on the Reef (up to 200 making their home on and around a single reef), and 350 different kinds of coral, more than one-third of all the coral species in the world.

UPPER LEFT: *After being touched, tiny polyps (telestacean) withdraw and leave only the hard external skeleton*
LOWER LEFT: *Michaelmas Cay*

But, having admired the most obvious of each reef's living creatures: the fish — and not forgetting that coral itself is a living creature — we have only just begun to discover its inhabitants. Shellfish, crabs, worms, anemones, sea urchins, stars, shrimps, jellyfish, sponges, and countless others also call these places home. The large predator fish: groper, tuna, and marlin, glide through these waters, with whales, sharks, dolphins, manta rays, octopus, and squid. Dugongs graze like underwater cattle on sea-grass beds, and no less than six of the world's seven species of sea turtles heave themselves up the sand to deposit millions of eggs in a season. Many islands and cays are the safe nesting-grounds for thousands of birds: gulls, frigate birds, tropic birds, Torres Strait pigeons, noddies, mutton birds, gannets, and many, many more.

The whole reef system is an amazing interaction of fragile relationships. Indeed, if it were not for a mutual assistance plan between two of the tiniest creatures of the reef, none of this mighty complex of living things could exist. Tiny single-celled plants called zooxanthellae, sheltering inside the tissue in the cylindrical creatures called polyps, and themselves feeding off the wastes exuded by the polyps, use the warm sun to manufacture the elements the polyps need to create the calcium from which reefs are built. Both the microscopic plant and the tiny animal need each other to survive. Their relationship provides the building blocks which are basic to the survival of this most wondrous and complex web of life on earth.

The incredible thing about both rainforests and reefs is that death plays such an important part in their foundation that we could call them the world's largest, yet most lived-in, graveyards. The reefs are made from the skeletal remains of millions of coral polyps. The rainforest is nourished by its own recycled droppings of leaves, twigs, and fruit; countless tiny bacteria

and micro-organisms act as a most efficient army of garbage-disposal experts on the forest floor!

Other fascinating life communities exist between the reef and the rainforest. The tidal forests we call mangroves, with their unique salt-shedding, oxygen-grabbing trees on stilt roots, are nurseries for many precious creatures, from the rich bounties of fish, crabs and prawns, to the amazing little mudskippers scurrying across mudflats with their water supply in their gills — and the awesome and dangerous salt-water crocodiles. The wallum sand country, so rich in wildflowers — grevillea, tea tree, heath, banksia — teems with honey-seeking birds and insects. Extensive wetlands and tidal mudflats bless areas around Cairns and Townsville with some of the world's best water-bird observing places. Any soft handful of feathers and bone which flies

halfway round the world each year to rendezvous at a particular swamp or mudflat deserves to be stared at with some respect!

But for all that, after the Reef, it is the rainforest which visitors most want to see. What they do see, of course, is only a glorious remnant of a once extensive, unique forest. The tropical forests of North Queensland are what many visitors expect all of Queensland to look like, and they are disappointed when it does not! Relative to the size of the original, these forests, mostly in mountainous areas, are small. The vast majority of the lowland rainforest was cleared for sugar farms, making that the rarest rainforest of all.

RIGHT: *An ancient survivor, Brampton Island*

optimum conditions for the lush growth of the closed forest systems we popularly call 'rainforest'. The mountains which trap the rainfall also produce the fast, voluminous forest streams which cascade down the bouldered passes, and plunge over some of Australia's most spectacular waterfalls, especially on the Atherton Tableland. The single, white 300-metre slash and roar of water which is Wallaman Falls, near Ingham, is one of the highest in the world.

Forests, like reefs, vary immensely from one to the other. The ever-dripping forests down from the mountain summits, swathed in an almost continuous cloak of swirling mists, differ markedly from the steamy tropical jungles of the lowland. Yet all true rainforests feature tall trees with interlocking crowns which greatly restrict light to a second or third layer of under-storey plants. Occasionally, like a Martin Luther King or a Gandhi in the human realm, one forest giant will tower over all the others. Such giants are true wonders, some estimated to be 3,500 years old. In fact, the overall high proportion of the world's 'primitive flowering plants' in the North Queensland forests leads many scientists to postulate that these may well be the oldest forests on earth!

In true rainforest, so little light filters down that the vegetation on the forest floor is quite open, consisting of smaller under-storey shrubs, seedlings waiting patiently for their turn to spear up to any break in the canopy, and mosses, ferns, lichens, and fungi. Another

The amount of rain that falls in North Queensland is legendary, most of it drumming onto the coastal ranges in the summer months of December to March. The 'wet gumboot' towns of Innisfail, Tully, and Babinda measure their annual rainfall in metres! This immense rainfall, high year-round temperatures and humidity, and the deep red basalt soils, create

large family of ferns, orchids, and mosses — among them the well-known staghorns and elkhorns, bird's-nest and hare's-foot ferns — are known as epiphytes, and colonise cliffs and the trunks and branches of trees. Up to 50 different such plants have been found pick-a-backing on a single forest tree. As well, giant lianas and vines, as thick as a man, snake to the very tops of the canopy, and festoon large areas of forest with curtains of cascading greenery.

But it is the trees themselves that the visitor notices first. Though there are 1,200 different species of trees in these forests, to the untrained eye they often appear similar to each other. Many have giant buttresses and long, snaking surface roots. Their trunks are usually smooth, tall, and straight — except for the criss-crossing lattice-work of the strangler fig. Their leaves, most often large, soft, and bright green (as compared with the greys of wattles and gum trees) feature pronounced 'drip tips' for shedding water.

In these cool, moist cathedrals, where many of the 'pillars of the church' have not even been named yet, lives the richest array of wildlife on earth, apart from the tropical reefs. Yet, because the forest and its ways are alien to us, we rarely sight much of that wildlife. In the forest clearings and margins, we do frequently see in flashing, erratic flight the two crown jewels of Australian butterflies: the green and black Cairns Birdwing, and the cornflower Blue Ulysses. Tree kangaroos, rodents, bats, and the beautiful 'leaping possums' called lemuroids, move around the treetops, along with ringtail and brushtail possums, and the strange,

slower, seldom-sighted cuscus. Most rainforest trees bear fleshy fruits, and a myriad of birds, flying foxes, and native mammals pays for the privilege of feasting on that fruit by distributing the seeds, complete with little dobs of fertilizer, away from the host tree! The magnificent flightless, helmeted cassowary, and the mound-building scrub turkeys and jungle fowl, gorge themselves on the fallen fruit. So rich is the food supply, and so short the time needed to satisfy oneself for a day, that many of the birds, such as the birds of paradise (or riflebirds) and the bowerbirds, spend a great deal of their days displaying themselves and dancing in elaborate mate-attracting rituals, often performing on specially constructed, intricate platforms.

The human history of North Queensland, as with most of Australia, recedes into the mists of antiquity. It is known that Aboriginal people inhabited parts of the rainforest and some reef islands

for longer than white people can even imagine. What useful knowledge those people had of these areas, and what a vast treasure store of uses they found for the flora and fauna! Some Aborigines still retain some knowledge of nature's food and medicine from the sea, and especially from the forest. It is imperative that what is still known by our black brothers and sisters be carefully recorded for the sake of all, and no less for the sake of these special places themselves.

The coming of the white man's so-called civilization is always a two-sided coin: many benefits, and many losses. With the white man and his way of life arrived a violence that the land had known previously only in the greatest of the natural calamities. The lowland forests were cut and burnt for sugar cane. Other areas were torn apart for gold and mineral riches. The precious cabinet timbers of the forest: cedar, maple, black bean, were extracted by hard-toiling loggers. Australia's very own slave

trade, called 'blackbirding', flourished. Whole tribes of Aborigines disappeared. Diggers of many races, including Chinese, died in clashes on the Palmer River goldfields. Hundreds of Japanese pearl-shell divers perished from 'the bends'. And time and again, cyclones whirled in from the Pacific to devastate whole natural and human communities.

Today, in what is arguably the most decentralized of all the Australian States, moderately sized cities flourish along the narrow coastal strip separating the Reef from the remaining rainforest. Thousands of people, either directly or indirectly, make their living from one or the other. It was inevitable, then, given today's growing concern for the natural wonders of the world, that both the Reef and the rainforest should become environmental battlegrounds. Extremes on both sides of the battle, it seemed, would not desist until the whole area was either totally despoiled and exploited, or totally locked away from human

interference. The battle has been largely resolved (though naturally not to the satisfaction of all) through the creation of two huge World Heritage areas which encompass much of the forest and pretty well all of the Reef.

A new breeze is blowing in this part of Australia. Once, every farmer burnt his cane to remove the trash before harvesting. Now, a growing number cut the cane green, and return the trash to soil once nourished by the fallen forest litter. Perhaps one day the mighty cane fires will themselves pass entirely into folk-lore. By then, few Australians will question the wisdom of those who placed the remaining great forests and the Reef on the list of the World Heritage, and set them aside in perpetuity as playgrounds where people of all nations may come to marvel, and to be recreated, enfolded in these gifts of the Creator's grace, so absolutely special.

MORNING ON THE ESTUARY

Someone opened
the veins of a sleeping land,
bleeding gold
onto burnished sand.

LEFT: *Daintree River*
UPPER RIGHT: *Sunrise, Florence Bay, Magnetic Island*
LOWER RIGHT: *Sunrise, Tully Heads*

IN YOUR PRESENCE

Thank you, Father, for
these lazy days,
eternal summer,
butterflies, starfish, clams,
green waterfalls of forest trees
tumbling down mountains,
spilling out onto golden sand:
green-and-gold Queensland,
Australia.

How can the thought of you
be no more than
that unrecognisable speck
(presumably a boat)
on the endless horizon
of shimmering blue?

You are everywhere;
your scent, the unseen frangipanni
breathed by a holy breeze
over everything.

LEFT: *View from Passage Peak, Hamilton Island*
UPPER RIGHT: *The giant clam* (tridacna gigas)
CENTRE RIGHT: *Red sea star* (fromia elegans)
FAR RIGHT: *White frangipanni*

OF GOD AND SAND

The unfathomable mystery
of a grain of sand:
that God is
that tiny cell
which surrounds, enfolds, encloses,
the entire universe,
but is surrounded, enfolded,
    enclosed,
in a single grain
of fine beach sand. *

If I could understand
that secret of that one grain of sand,
then I would know
how God could become a Man.

Based on words of Martin Luther

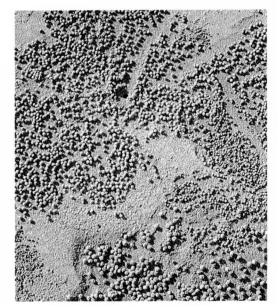

UPPER LEFT: *Pandanus palm, Bushy Atoll*
LOWER LEFT: *Balgal Beach*
UPPER RIGHT: *A red gorgonia fan coral (melithaea squamata)
and some feather starfish catch the current*
LOWER RIGHT: *Hundreds of tiny coral polyps (telestacean)
form a gorgonia fan coral*

SHALLOW WATERS

God,
if warmth and shallowness
in the tropic seas
are your prerequisites
for the flowering of corals
as beautiful as these —
then eliminate from me
all coldness
toward you and your creatures,
and any false pride
in the depth of my thinking,
so that my life too
might produce
such prolific beauty.

THE MISSION

Search and enjoy!
Scour this land
in search of its Creator,
like writers
raiding the world
for images,
flying foxes
ransacking the forest
for blossom and fruit!

UPPER LEFT: *White sapote, tropical fruit*
LOWER LEFT: *Rainbow lorikeets enjoy a*
flowering umbrella tree
RIGHT: *Kirrama Range, Cardwell Shire*

THE GREATEST MYSTERY

Einstein said that
the greatest mystery of the universe
was that we can know it.
Mystery, wonder, and privilege —
all blended into one!
Yet there is a mystery
surpassing Einstein's greatest:
that God became a Man
so that, within this universe,
we might know
our Maker,
and knowing him,
respond with love for him
in the care of what he has made.

UPPER LEFT: *An egg cowrie* (ovula ovum) *feeding on soft coral*
LOWER LEFT: *The beauty of golden daisy polyps* (tubastraea aurea)
is best displayed at night time
RIGHT: *Sunrise, Balgal Beach*
OVERLEAF: *A coral wall drop-off with a coral cod* (cephalopholis
minatus) *in the foreground*

UPPER LEFT: *A group of miniature yellow sea squirts* (ecteinascidia nexa)
LOWER LEFT: *A* clownfish (amphiprion ocellaris covier) *peers*
through the tentacles of its host anemone
UPPER RIGHT: *Red fan coral* (ctenocella pectinata)
LOWER RIGHT: *Lace coral* (stylaster elegans)

REEF

This is a field
where all the players
from all the teams
of all the games,
with all their supporters,
have come to rage together
in one bewildering kaleidoscope
of colour, movement, shape, beauty.

Here 'I am forever bound
to be a spectator on life,
never a player'. *

Colour assaults the eye,
every conceivable shade,
the entire spectrum unfolding,
flowering, exploding:
translucent pink, yellow, orange,
red, purple, silver, blue.

Movement blurs the mind,
every choreographed turn,
from the languid predators,
lazy, large,
to the jitterbug, zip-away prey:
the scurrying, pulsating, clinging,
spiralling, darting, waving
extravagance of reef.

Spectators don't play;
they cheer!
Well done, great God, well done!

* C.S. Lewis

DETRITUS

Sometimes
when the tide recedes,
I discover
the most beautiful things,
stranded.

Why, God,
do I find it so hard
to see the same beauty
in those people
whom life has left behind?

TEMPTATION

Father God,
watch over my love
for these wild places
whose incomparable beauty
overpowers me.
I could stay here forever,
in love with a lifestyle,
playing with my toys,
soaking up this
abundance of freedom,
abandoning all responsibility
toward you, family, friends,
and the suffering poor.

Thank you for refreshment
given to me here.
Let me return recreated
to my place of work
to enflesh your love
in the not-so-pretty setting
of daily routine,
without forest, sea-breeze, and surf.

UPPER LEFT: *Goats, Lindeman Island*
LOWER LEFT: *Yacht race, Hamilton Island*
UPPER RIGHT: *View across Butterfly Valley, Lindeman Island*
LOWER RIGHT: *Sunrise, Hamilton Island*

MANGROVE FOREST

God of my life,
when I struggle
to grasp the purpose
in the endless cycle
of my life's gains and losses,
let me see the truth
you have stored
in the maze of the mangroves.

There, at the interface
of land and sea,
you have shaped this marvel
of a seemingly changeless place,
built on the rise and fall of tides,
the in-and-out flow of nutrients,
the traffic of living and dead.

Show me
the same pattern at work in me,
a piece of permanence
shaped from the flux
of people, events, and things,
a spawning place for life
and creativity.

LEFT: *Mangroves, Myall Beach, Cape Tribulation*
RIGHT: *Mangroves, Cape York*

ILLUSION

A paradise wrapped in such beauty
and seeming peace
beguiles like a serpent:
If only we lived here,
all would be well!

Yet living well
is a matter of the heart,
not of place;
of how we live,
not where.

It is an illusion to think
that the good life
is always somewhere else,
perhaps where it's more sunny,
or the mother-in-law won't call!

No place is more favoured
than God's gift
of the place we are now.

But places are also for leaving,
and arriving at.
If he should move you
someplace else,
then go happily —
as to an adventure,
a new discovery.

In that spirit
he leads you
place by place
to his Father's house.

It will be well
wherever you go
with him.

SUNRISE CONFESSION

It's the stuff of postcards,
all this burnished liquid gold,
the dark world transformed,
awakening.

I confess I would rather
see such miracles out there
than here within.

Who wants to be
created again?
Who wants you, God,
breaking through,
flooding in?

Do I intrude on you?

Why can't you
stay put in the churches,
let me grub along being human,
and I'll just drop by,
if I decide to, one day. *

** Based on words of Dale Kohler,
from a John Updike novel*

UPPER LEFT: *Sunrise, Tully Heads*
LOWER LEFT: *Early morning, Arthur Bay, Magnetic Island*
UPPER RIGHT: *Coconut palms, Bramston Beach*
LOWER RIGHT: *Shepherd's Beach, Hinchinbrook Island*
OVERLEAF: *Junk, Long Island*

AT SCHOOL WITH FISH

God,
weak as I am,
I am prone to be swallowed alive.
Teach me the prudence
of swimming in the school
of your family.

Lord,
teach me the lesson of the puffer fish:
that, if I blow myself up
to make others feel small,
I am full of hot air,
and poisonous.

Lord, does the cleaner wrasse,
swimming right inside the shark's
  mouth
to pick clean the teeth and gills,
feel as insecure as I when
doing business with predators?

LEFT: A *school of strippers* (lutjanus carponotatus)
UPPER RIGHT: An *epaulette shark* (hemiscyllium ocellatum)
MIDDLE RIGHT: A *minky whale swims by*
LOWER RIGHT: A *large nudibranch* (notodoris gardineri)
feeding on algae

People with evil intent,
who imitate the genuinely good,
learn their ways from false cleaner
    fish:
looking and acting like cleaners,
allowed to swim up close,
they open their jaws
and rip off lumps of flesh!

Jonah wouldn't believe it, God!
This mighty 15 tonnes and 18
    metres
of grey gliding whale shark,
the largest shark alive,
is gulping, for breakfast,
plankton so small that
Jonah could hardly see them!

O my God,
now there's a pearlfish,
at home inside the gut
of molluscs or sea slugs,
slipping out at night to feed!
Is there no end
to your ability
to stun us?

NATURE

I am nature;
please pause to understand me.

I am, like you,
a creature —
your sister, not your God.

Expect of me
what you would of God,
and we will destroy each other.

For love of our common Creator,
walk kindly with me,
for I have neither capacity
for endless renewal,
nor innate ability
to forgive you
endlessly.

UPPER LEFT: *The delicate colours of the teddy bear coral tree (dendronephthya) are most revealing at night*
LOWER LEFT: *Delicate heart fan corals (ctenocella pectinata) grow in lower depths of some 20 metres or more*
UPPER RIGHT: *The gills of the spiral tube worm or Christmas tree worm extend from its protective hard coral surrounding (spirobranchus giganteus)*
LOWER RIGHT: *The giant triton shell (charonia tritonis)*

THE GROUND AT MY FEET

Lord God,
remember that day
I discovered a flame tree
blazing above the forest canopy
by spent flower cinders
lying among the pillars
on the forest floor?

And remember
how I first saw white water
breaking on the reef offshore
after I found
that bit of broken coral
on the beach?

How many previous times
did you pepper my path
with pointers
to higher and wider things,
and I never knew,
having forgotten to stoop,
to stare at the earth
where I placed my feet?

LEFT: *Hardy Reef, Great Barrier Reef*
UPPER RIGHT: *Seashore creeper, Balgal Beach*
LOWER RIGHT: *Plantation Beach, Lindeman Island*

TO OVERCOME FEAR

'He was in the desert 40 days,
being tempted by Satan.
He was with the wild animals,
*and angels attended him.' ***

Lord Jesus Christ,
you walked with wild animals
in their own domain,
angels watching over you:
Please plunge with me now
into the great deep
where the grey swirl lurks,
the gaping mouth of terrible teeth,
the awful face, the eye.
Teach me to recognize
the beasts that snarl in me,
to accept them as part of me,
and to walk unafraid among them,
my hand in yours.

Lord of the great unexplored deep,
and of all wild things,
real or imagined:
swim with me
in those dark waters
which uphold, not drown,
when we swim without fear.

*** Mark 1:13 NIV*

CROWN OF THORNS

UPPER LEFT: *The porcupine fish (diodon holacanthus) and its protective spines*
LOWER LEFT: *The barracuda (agrioposphyraena barracuda) swims by*
RIGHT: *The crown of thorns starfish (acanthaster planci) feeding on coral polyps*

Take heart, little polyp,
your Maker too
wore a crown of thorns,
and lived!

He watches sparrows —
and you!

THE SCHOOL

A cloud of tiny fish
shimmered past,
a synchronised darting of thousands,
skipping for protection
among the corals.
How like the church,
that fellowship of the weak,
finding strength in companionship
under the eternal Rock.

UPPER LEFT: *A crinoid or feather starfish*
(comanthina nobilis) *relies on the currents for its food*
LOWER LEFT: *Male and female fairy bassett fish*
(anthias squammipinnis)
RIGHT: *A myriad of bait fish* (parapriacanthus
ransonneti) *hides from predators in a cave*

AFTER PSALM ONE

Blessed, and a blessing,
is that giant forest tree
towering up from roots
sipping cool mountain cascades.
Its vast shady canopy
creates a twilight world
for the softest fern,
safe from the burning
of the tropic sun.

UPPER LEFT: *Five-corner fruit, tropical fruit*
LOWER LEFT: *Possum, Magnetic Island*
NEARER RIGHT: *Sugar cane firing*
FAR RIGHT: *Kangaroo*
OVERLEAF: *Oyster Bay, Brampton Island*

Leaves drop,
a litter of nutrients;
blossoms burst in season;
fruit swells, and falls,
peppering the ground
like crumbs under the table
of a messy eater.
The feasters, day and night, gorge:
flying flox, possum, cassowary,
lorikeet, tree kangaroo, rat.

Wise as the wisest man,
rooted in the love of God,
this tree feeds from the spring
that never dries up —
blessed, and a blessing.

Down below, on the plain —
cursed, and a curse —
the smoke from the trash
in the burning cane
billows, belches, rolls
to the ozone,
descends on the beaches,
on white washing on the line,
like black sooty rain.

Such is the fate of the fool,
who spurns the very idea of God
and mocks the worshipper.
In his arrogance
he calls down a curse,
and himself falls like a blight
on the land.

UNDERSEA ALTAR

I feel like one
who has stepped
from a noisy street
into this holy place
of silent adoration.
Above me the wind,
the mewing of the gulls,
the throbbing of engines;
here, just the liturgical dance,
the banners,
the wordless Gloria!

UPPER LEFT: *A clump of miniature purple sea squirts*
(podoclavella moluccensis)
LOWER LEFT: *Game fishing boat, Cairns*
UPPER RIGHT: *A dancing black clownfish* (amphiprion
melanopus bleeker)
LOWER RIGHT: *A timid moray eel* (gymnothorax) *peers
from its protective hole*

FISH

Fish are just underwater birds
riding the currents like thermals.
When they die,
they spiral and tumble like leaves
falling to the ocean floor.
But the best of parrots
and autumn trees
never boasted such magnificence
of form and colour
as these.

CHOIR

Farmers burning off cane,
trawler men unloading prawns,
students tapping keyboards,
divers poring over minute data
gathered on the reef;

Mangrove forest crawling with
    crabs
and popping with mud;
wetlands playing host
to flocks of tourists
photographing terns and stilts;
mountains birthing rivulets,
wallum conceiving flowers —

Everything at work,
doing its natural best,
united in the diversity
of work as worship.

Suddenly I'm asking:
Please, God,
may I join in?

UPPER LEFT: *Cray fishing boat, Thursday Island*
LOWER LEFT: *Jabiru*
UPPER RIGHT: *Pink water lily*
LOWER RIGHT: *Sunrise, Hinchinbrook Island*

KILLING FIELDS

We choose reef and forest
as playgrounds of beauty,
serenity, and peace.
We come for refreshment, recrea-
  tion.

But then, there's a carpet snake
half through swallowing a possum,
or a pair of reef sharks
herding fish into the shallows,
and lo, the killing fields!
Eat and avoid being eaten,
kill or die!

For what purpose would God
so painstakingly paint
the minute scales of angel fish
or blue ulysses butterflies,
if they are mere links
in the long food-chain?

Faith, not at all squeamish
in the face of such realities,
declares:
    'You are God,
    alive in everything.
    Your hand always
    cradles your creatures,
    always leads each creature
    to that certain end
    for which you made it
    in power, wisdom, and love.

Everything is
as you designed
it should be.' *

Based on words of Julian of Norwich

UPPER LEFT: *Python*
LOWER LEFT: *Green Island, Cairns*
UPPER RIGHT: *A prowling lion fish* (pterois antennata)
LOWER RIGHT: *A white tip reef shark* (triaenodon obesus)

THE SONG

I imagined
this planet's future sounds,
hearing noise,
but no song.

We had
felled the forest,
quarried the mountain,
dammed every free-flowing stream,
made mangroves into roadways,
and wetlands into fairways,
smothered the reef
under blankets of red silt.

Made lots of jobs,
heaps of dough.
Killed the song.

Where will cassowary or cuscus go?
Where will flying fox, lorikeet
find blossom trees now?
Turtle plough the sand?
Crocodile guard her nest?
Where will you see, flashing by,
the blue and green gems of the sky:
ulysses, birdwing?

'Glory to God in the highest'?
Just the measured beat
of the hammer
nailing our sense of the sacred
to Mammon's door.

Lord, have mercy;
we made lots of jobs,
heaps of dough,
but killed the song.

UPPER LEFT: *Freshwater crocodile*
LOWER LEFT: *A giant green turtle* (chelonia mydas)

RIGHT: *Normanby River, Cape York*

BECOMING

Tiny, in the palm of his hand,
lies the Creator's recent work,
this vast complex of reef.
Who can say what God
will yet make from all this
quintessence of colour,
variety, life?

Long ago he made other reefs
as big and as wondrous as this.
Then, recalling the waters,
he pushed up their bones
as ranges in the desert,
limestone chains where eucalypts
    blossom
instead of sea anemones,
and wallaroos, not whales,
dunnarts, not dugongs,
come to play.

How little we know
how busily the Creator continues
his masterpiece still!

Vast, the sweep of his control,
wide, the embrace of his love,
hidden, the final strokes
of his brush on us!

Already now
the Mover of surf and wind
changes the furniture
of his home around;
this reef is being transformed
to something else.

And if it surpasses this,
move on, great God,
move on!

RETURNING

And will the great God come
to make us whole again?

Look! The trinity
of the boundless Deep,
wind, wave, and tide,
combine to recreate the place
when feet have marked the sand.

Truly,
our great God has come,
and comes, like waves,
again, again, again.

UPPER LEFT: *Wattle, Cape York*
LOWER LEFT: *Tully Gorge, Cardwell Shire, North Queensland*
UPPER RIGHT: *Koala, Nature Reserve, Hamilton Island*
LOWER RIGHT: *Plantation Beach, Lindeman Island*
OVERLEAF: *Silhouetted diver near a coral wall drop off*

GOD OF SMALL THINGS

God of the broad vista,
the panoramic view,
the wide-angle lens:
do not allow our obsession
with big things —
big ideas, big projects, big
    money —
to blind us to appreciation
of small wonders,
minute marvels,
precious details.

God of all stories, great and small,
teach us the story of small things;
of plankton at the start
of the chain of food
which feeds the world;
of polyps constructing
one on another
earth's largest living home;
of the hidden bacteria
recycling an entire forest floor.

Let us not hold
as of no consequence
any of your small ones,
including ourselves,
in a universe where
one tiny Baby's birth
in a borrowed cowshed
is the smallest story
ever to change an entire world.

UPPER LEFT: *The gills of the spiral tube worm or
Christmas tree worm extend from its protective hard coral
surrounding* (spirobranchus giganteus)
LOWER LEFT: *A crinoid or feather starfish*
(himerometra robustipinna) *feeding on microscopic
organisms*
UPPER RIGHT: *Langford Reef, Whitsunday Passage*
LOWER RIGHT: *A tiny coral shrimp takes shelter in
an anemone*

LIKE CORAL, LIKE FISH

Hold no illusions
about your beauty or strength.
You are like dazzling reef fish,
like the glorious reef itself.
See how the coral pales,
the little fish turn grey
so soon,
when the water of life
is taken away.

You are like coral and fish.
Strength withers,
beauty fades.

Only the Word of God
stands strong and lovely
forever. *

* After Isaiah 40:6–8

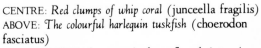

CENTRE: *Red clumps of whip coral* (junceella fragilis)
ABOVE: *The colourful harlequin tuskfish* (choerodon fasciatus)
CENTRE RIGHT: *An attractive butterfly cod* (pterois volitans) *displays its poisonous spines*
FAR RIGHT: *Reef, Bushy Atoll*

WORLD HERITAGE

I thank you, God,
for the concept of world heritage:
among all your gifts to us,
some rank so special
that only crass greed
or rank selfishness
would prevent our sharing them
with the whole world —
places entrusted to Australians
for the wonder of all people.

But lest our vision of heritage,
even in this vast land,
should become too small,
keep reminding us
that, without knowledge of you,
our true inheritance
has already slipped away,
and we have pitifully little
to share.

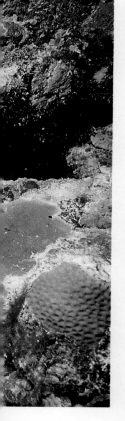

FOR A RIGHT MIND

Guard, O God,
the springs of my mind,
and its estuary, my lips,
lest, like a wet season torrent,
I pour out
an endless stream
of detritus.

UPPER LEFT: *Sunrise, Hinchinbrook Island*
LOWER LEFT: *Rain clouds, Cairns*
RIGHT: *Waterfall, Cedar Creek, Airlie Beach*

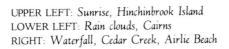

THE MUSIC OF RAIN

One sultry summer day,
way back when
Babinda, Tully, Innisfail
hadn't yet been born —
God, noticing the bored
faces of his favourite frogs,
clapped his hands at the sky:
'Music!' God shouted,
'Let's have some music to dance by!'

The sky, wishing to oblige,
yet not wanting to admit
it knew nothing about tunes,
decided instead to make it rain.

It rolled in the mighty cloud-heads,
the billowing sons of Monsoon;
thunderbolts clapped in tune,
and winds whipped and slapped
a quickening refrain.

And it rained, rained,
and it rained!
It drummed on the mountains,
drummed on the cane,
drummed sheet on sheet
on the waterlogged plain.
It pattered and spattered
the broad forest leaves,
tapped on farm windows,
spilled over farm eaves.
It dribbled and chortled
down hillsides;
crashed and thrashed
through bouldered ravines;
hurtled off cliff-tops
in long white-ribboned roars;
smashed itself down
to the deep valley floors.
And high on the summits,
where mists swirl and slink,
it whispered like tears
down the faces of rocks,
and dripped,
plink ... plink ... plink.

And the anxious sky asked:
'Well, what do you think?'

The frogs had never heard
such music before!
They rasped and hooted
and plonked applause;
and God, in the absence of sun,
beamed.

Ever since, each summer,
when the mangoes ripen,
and boredom settles like sleep
on those three sugar towns,
the sky cracks open with rain,
a million frogs applaud,
the walls don coats of mildew,
and God pulls his dancing
gumboots on!

OUT OF OUR DEPTH

We are aliens on the Reef, for sure!
People out of our depth!
Look how we struggle,
fumble for handles,
words to catalogue
so many strange and wonderful fish!
We name them
after things we know
in our dry-land world.

Consider this list:
Batfish, catfish, cowfish, goatfish,
parrot-, butterfly-, hawk-, angelfish,
pipe-, stone-, box-, trumpetfish,
scorpion-, wasp-, toad-, devilfish,
surgeon-, cardinal, angler, emperor!

If we wrestle with words
for our neighbouring watery world,
how totally at sea
will our floundering minds be
trying to imagine
worlds beyond this one,
to which one day,
by the grace of God,
we are called to go.

What poor pictures
from our world
we impose
on his!

Love him then,
and live with what you have:
the promise of his presence,
assurance of his love.

One day
you'll see him
as he is.

UPPER LEFT: *A manta ray* (manta alfredi)
LOWER LEFT: *A clown triggerfish* (balistoides conspicillus)
UPPER RIGHT: *A large batfish* (platax teira)
LOWER RIGHT: *Delicate patterns on a teddy bear coral tree* (dendronephthya)

AND WHEN I DIE, LORD JESUS

LEFT: *Sunset, Hayman Island*
UPPER RIGHT: *Balgal Beach*
LOWER RIGHT: *Balgal Beach*
OVERLEAF: *Hardy Reef, Great Barrier Reef*

Sweep away the fear
that drains me,
as sudden rain
sweeps heavy humidity
from the weary day.

And gather me
to rest in you,
as drops are gathered
into the safe folds
of the welcoming sea.

UNLESS YOU REACH OUT

The ocean, vast, unending,
outstretching the eye's power
to see its breakers
on some faraway shore,
hints to us of eternity.

We are fishes out of water,
born to drown in such a tide,
unless you reach out your hand
to lift us into your boat,
there to enjoy
eternity's waters,
already on earth.

NEW BIRTHRIGHT

Lord God,
when I hear you call
heaven your throne,
and earth your footstool, *
I picture you relaxing
in places like this,
on holidays, with your feet up,
soaking up your sun.

And when I read your promise
that, along with Jesus, freely given,
you graciously give us all things, **
I rejoice that all this beauty
is my heritage,
not by right of my birth
as an Australian,
but of my new birth
into your kingdom.

So, when I come here,
like you, to relax,
I come in a spirit of worship,
to have you recreate me
by your presence in this paradise,
where you teach me again
the holy arts of Sabbath:
to be humble and grateful,
to wonder and praise.

Isaiah 60:1
**Romans 8:32*

UPPER LEFT: *Picnic Bay, Magnetic Island*
LOWER LEFT: *Stinging hydroid* (aglaeophenia cupressina) *often catches the unsuspecting snorkeller with its painful sting*
UPPER RIGHT: *Sunrise, Bramston Beach*
LOWER RIGHT: *An arrow crab* (naxioides mammillata) *taking a walk on teddy bear coral*

PEACE

'The tenseness of twentieth-
    century living ebbs
when looking over the pale green sea
and feeling at one with the great rhythms
of sun, moon, and the winds.' *

Of course!
But that is just one dimension
of the iceberg of reality.
The Breath of all things
in, with, and under this world
of earth, air, fire, and water,
moves as he will, unseen.

To neglect such a place as this
would indeed be foolish,
but to ignore the reality
of the Spirit of this place,
without whom nothing can be,
would be to lose what peace we have.

'Don't seek peace in little things
in which there is no rest;
recognize your true rest in God,
all-powerful, all-wise, all-good,
for what is less than God
will never be enough for you.' **

* *Reader's Digest Book of the Great Barrier Reef, 43*
** *Based on words of Julian of Norwich*

UPPER LEFT: *Orchid Beach, Hinchinbrook Island*
LOWER LEFT: *Turtle Bay, Brampton Island*
RIGHT: *Moonrise, Cardwell Beach*

LIKE A CRAB IN ITS SHELL

Allow me, Lord Jesus,
the gift of your peace —
that I might
carry it about with me,
and retreat into it
when the tide turns,
like a crab
in its shell.

UPPER LEFT: *Crab hides under a rock, Balgal Beach*
LOWER LEFT: *Blubber jellyfish floating in the current*
UPPER RIGHT: *Pink lace coral* (stylaster elegans) *is very delicate, and grows in caves or under coral overhangs*
LOWER RIGHT: *A yellow corkscrewed whip coral* (cirripathes spiralis)

ALREADY NOW

Father,
in the world to come,
will you call us to account
for all the beauty
you put on earth,
which we never saw?

Look around you, my child!
What makes you think
I'll wait till eternity
to send out accounts?

MEETING

Meeting
is the act
for making old worlds
new.

A seed meets
the soil
to make a tree;
a stream meets
the shore
and becomes the sea;
a man meets
a woman
to create a family.

Wherever
this meeting of two
makes something new,
an unseen Love
shapes their embrace,
unseen lips
join the lips
of those two:
'Let there be!'

Look, said Jesus,
I make everything new —
even you.

LEFT: *Daintree River*
UPPER RIGHT: *Turtles, Cairns, Great Barrier Reef*
LOWER RIGHT: *Tree, Oyster Bay, South Molle Island*

AFFLUENCE

True affluence
is needing nothing
but the God of all grace
and supply.

Be careful
when you take the path
which leads downhill.
It is always much easier
to keep going
than to turn back.

Loving money, somebody said,
is like drinking seawater:
the more you drink,
the more you want —
and eventually
it kills you.

VISION

Of all gifts,
the greatest is the vision
to read the signs
in God's artwork,
and to recognize him
alive in all the universe,
and all the universe
alive in him.

Such vision begins
all wisdom,
wonder,
and love.

LEFT: *Delicate patterns of small delicate corals*
UPPER RIGHT: *Ribbon worms (baseodiscus quinquelineatus)*
generally found on coral/sandy seabed, have much the same function as earthworms
LOWER RIGHT: *The sea squirt (didemnum molle) filters water*
through tiny holes around the outside and into the centre
OVERLEAF: *Beautiful pink teddy bear soft coral (dendronephthya)*

POSTCARD

'Having the time of my life',
she wrote,
and I took her words
as warning.

My days melt away
like water on sand.
The great ocean
draws me to itself.
Rise, go to work, die.

Let me be careful of time, my God,
for these are the only
earthly days I own.

I too am having
the time of my life,
and I wish I had
more wisdom!

LEFT: *Moonlight, South Molle Island*
UPPER RIGHT: *Cardwell jetty and beach*
LOWER RIGHT: *Bushy Atoll*

SABBATH

Loving God,
you gave us the emerald sea,
the great rhythms
of sun, tide, wind,
and used the seventh day to relax
and enjoy what you made:
teach us too to live
within rhythms of ebb and flow.

Make us cherish the wisdom of quiet rest
after a hard day's work,
the holiness of holiday,
and the futility of toiling endlessly —
even for you —
as if exhaustion were a virtue,
and busyness next to godliness.

Teach us to treasure 'useless' time,
when nothing is produced,
or repaired, or cleaned,
but our tired bodies and minds
are refreshed
in earth's quiet places
where you too rest,
delighting in your work.

LEFT: *Hinchinbrook Channel, Hinchinbrook Island*
RIGHT: *Palms in sunset, Brampton Island*

GOD OF THE EBB AND FLOW

God of life's ebb and flow:
yours is the dying,
the rising, yours.
You sow in sorrow,
and harvest in joy.

God of the cycles,
sunset, sunrise,
living or dying,
I am yours.

LEFT: *Yellow teddy bear tree coral (dendronephthya)*
RIGHT: *Sunrise, Balgal Beach*
OVERLEAF: *Hardy Reef, Great Barrier Reef*